ELIZABETH

VAN LEW

CIVIL WAR SPY

SPECIAL LIVES IN HISTORY THAT BECOME

Signature LIVES

ELIZABETH

VAN LEW

CIVIL WAR SPY

by Heidi Schoof

Content Adviser: DeAnne Blanton, Military Archivist,
National Archives and Records Administration,
Washington, D.C.

Reading Adviser: Rosemary G. Palmer, Ph.D.,
Department of Literacy, College of Education,
Boise State University

COMPASS POINT BOOKS ✦ MINNEAPOLIS, MINNESOTA

Compass Point Books
3109 West 50th Street, #115
Minneapolis, MN 55410

Visit Compass Point Books on the Internet at *www.compasspointbooks.com*
or e-mail your request to *custserv@compasspointbooks.com*

Editor: Sue Vander Hook
Lead Designer: Jaime Martens
Page Production: Bobbie Nuytten
Photo Researchers: Kelly Garvin and Svetlana Zhurkin
Cartographer: XNR Productions, Inc.
Educational Consultant: Diane Smolinski

Managing Editor: Catherine Neitge
Creative Director: Keith Griffin
Editorial Director: Carol Jones

Library of Congress Cataloging-in-Publication Data
Schoof, Heidi
  Elizabeth Van Lew / by Heidi Schoof
    p. cm—(Signature lives)
  Includes bibliographical references and index.
ISBN 0-7565-0985-8 (hardcover)
  1. Van Lew, Elizabeth L., 1818–1900—Juvenile literature. 2. United
States—History—History—Civil War, 1861-1865—Secret service—
Juvenile literature. 3. Spies—United States—Biography—Juvenile litera-
ture. 4. Women spies—United States—Biography—Juvenile literature.
I. Title. II. Series.
  E608.V34S36 2006
  973.7'85'092—dc22   2005003255

CIVIL WAR ERA

The Civil War (1861–1865) split the United States into two countries and divided the people over the issue of slavery. The opposing sides—the Union in the North and the Confederacy in the South—battled each other for four long years in the deadliest American conflict ever fought. The bloody war sometimes pitted family members and friends against each other over the issues of slavery and states' rights. Some of the people who lived and served their country during the Civil War are among the nation's most beloved heroes.

Elizabeth Van Lew

Table of Contents

1 GRAVEDIGGERS

❧❧❧

In a cemetery on the outskirts of Richmond, Virginia, an old gravedigger waited in the dark. It was almost midnight on that stormy, cold night in April 1864.

Martin Lipscomb, Frederick Lohmann, and his brother John slowly approached in their mule-drawn wagon. A grim and dangerous task was ahead of them. They knew the consequences—certain death—if they were caught.

The men were there to steal a body, the remains of 22-year-old Colonel Ulric Dahlgren, a brave officer in the Union Army. They had been sent on this mission by the leader of their spy network—Elizabeth Van Lew.

Without hesitation, the gravedigger led them to

Dahlgren's unmarked shallow grave. He knew right where it was. He had been there hiding behind a tree the night Confederate soldiers buried the young soldier. The men worked quickly, thankful for the claps of thunder and gusts of wind that covered up the noise they were making. Soon they unearthed a plain wooden coffin and pried open the lid.

First, they made sure it was Dahlgren's body. It was easy to identify—his right leg was missing. Less than a year before, he had lost his leg from injuries he received at the Battle of Gettysburg, Pennsylvania, one of the fiercest battles of the Civil War. He was fitted with a wooden leg—a costly item at the time. He continued to lead his soldiers in this war in which Americans were fighting Americans. Dahlgren's wooden leg wasn't in the coffin, however. The Confederate soldiers who killed him had taken it as well as one of his fingers.

Quickly, the men loaded the coffin into the back of their wagon and covered it up with burlap sacks. They cautiously made their way through rutted back streets of Richmond and headed to William S. Rowley's farm. Van Lew had told them to take the body there, to the home of a fellow spy. It was a safe place to hide the body until she arrived.

At the farm, the men took the coffin off the wagon and placed it in a shed, where Rowley sat with it all night. In the morning, Van Lew arrived with other members of her spy organization, called the Richmond Union Underground. After examining the body to make sure it was Dahlgren's, Van Lew helped transfer it carefully to a new metal coffin and load it on the back of a farm wagon. Rowley covered the coffin with about a dozen peach trees packed tightly around it. He was ready to take this special cargo to Robert Orrick's farm just outside Richmond for a secret burial. But first, he had to get past Confederate soldiers.

As Rowley approached a Southern checkpoint,

Richmond, Virginia, just before the Civil War

he noticed that soldiers were examining everything in the wagons ahead of him. However, he was acquainted with the man who came over to inspect his wagon, and they struck up a conversation about peach trees. Distracted, the soldier let Rowley go by without disturbing the peach trees.

Once Dahlgren's body was buried on Orrick's farm, Van Lew wrote a report of the incident in a secret message. As she had done so many times before, she wrote in code so Confederate soldiers would not be able to read it. The Dahlgren mission was completed, but Van Lew would go on to carry out many more dangerous tasks. She would become known as one of the most exceptional, clever spies of the Civil War.

Van Lew was not the only spy during the war. Thousands of people carried out secret assignments for both sides. They came from all walks of life, including farmers, slaves, merchants, soldiers, actresses, and wealthy ladies. Secret agents were all over the country, and some of the most effective ones were women.

Many women served as spies for both sides during the Civil War. They had several advantages over their male counterparts. Most people did not suspect women of secret activities, so soldiers often allowed them to travel across enemy lines without being questioned or searched. The female fashions of that time also made it easier for women spies. They could hide documents, secret messages, food, and medical supplies under their huge hooped skirts or in one of the many layers of their petticoats. Their food baskets sometimes concealed important papers or military orders.

Back view of a typical woman's fashion of the 1860s, with full hooped skirt and decorative ruffles

Although she lived in Richmond, Virginia, the capital of the Confederate states, Van Lew did not support the Confederate cause. She especially did not support slavery, one of the issues that was dividing the North and the South. In fact, she worked to free slaves and purchased many of them in order to grant them their freedom. Many former slaves even became effective members of her spy team.

Van Lew agreed with President Abraham Lincoln, although he was not popular in the South. She shared his view that slavery was wrong and agreed with him that the states should stay together as one country. Van Lew was committed to her principles, and she often risked her life to carry them out. She worked hard to accomplish what she believed was right, spending most of her money and sacrificing good relations with her Southern friends and neighbors along the way. Van Lew was good at what she did; some called her brilliant.

General Ulysses S. Grant, commander of the Union Army, highly valued her work as a spy. The messages she delivered to him were some of the most valuable information he received and helped him ultimately lead the Union to victory. Her messages were written in cipher, a code she created to conceal the meaning of correspondence and information about Confederate plans of attack. Throughout the war and until her death in 1900, she carried the small piece of paper that contained her code in her watch case.

When Grant became president of the United States after the war, he didn't forget Elizabeth Van Lew and put her in charge of the post office at Richmond. On a trip to Richmond with his wife, Grant insisted they stop by Van Lew's home. He wanted to visit the woman who had done such a great service for her country.

GLEASONS
PICTORIAL
L.L.SMITH

2 SOUTHERN GIRL

❧❦❧

Elizabeth Van Lew was 43 years old when the Civil War began in 1861. By 1862, she was doing spy work, smuggling messages to captured Union officers in a Richmond prison and taking information to Northern generals. But her life in Richmond, Virginia, had not always been so full of secrecy, intrigue, and undercover work.

In fact, when she was born in Richmond on October 15, 1818, her life was quiet and peaceful. Richmond was a simple town located 120 miles (192 kilometers) south of Washington, D.C., the nation's capital. About 6,000 people lived there in homes scattered over the countryside and along the James River. Horse-drawn carriages traveled along rutted roads, carrying people wherever they needed to go.

Just a few years before Elizabeth was born, stage-coaches began stopping regularly in Richmond to take people and goods to other cities along their interstate routes. In 1815, steamboats on the James River started docking at the Richmond port on a regular basis.

Richmond was the capital of the state of Virginia and the center of political life. History had been made in this city, where Patrick Henry delivered his famous "Give me liberty or give me death" speech in 1775. George Washington, the first president of the United States, had developed the area along the James River and Kanawha Canal. Thomas Jefferson, writer of the Declaration of Independence and third president of the United States, had designed the cor-

Logs were transported by boat on the James River through Richmond, Virginia.

nerstone of the state Capitol building. Washington, Jefferson, and James Madison, the fourth president of the United States, had all been born in the beautiful state of Virginia.

Elizabeth's ancestors were not from Virginia, however. Her father, John Van Lew, was from Long Island, New York, where he had lived with his Dutch family. His parents wanted him to become a college professor who taught the Latin language, but Van Lew was interested in retail stores. As a young man, he worked as an apprentice for a New York City merchant and learned how to manage and run a store. In 1816, he moved to Richmond, where he started a business with Dr. John Adams. Unfortunately, their business was not successful, and Van Lew was left with a $100,000 debt. He started another business—a hardware store—that proved to be successful, and he paid back all the money he owed. His store was the only one of its kind in the area, and people came from all over to buy tools and equipment there.

In Richmond, John Van Lew met Eliza Louise Baker, the daughter of Hilary Baker, the former mayor of Philadelphia, Pennsylvania. Eliza never knew her father, since he died of yellow fever three months before she was born. But she knew that he had been a committed patriot during the Revolutionary War (1775-1783). Just a year after the

In the 1800s, people called abolitionists worked to put an end to slavery. In 1831, William Lloyd Garrison published a Boston, Massachusetts, newspaper called The Liberator *to tell the U.S. Congress and the world that slavery must be abolished. A slave named Sojourner Truth, who was freed in 1827, began speaking publicly about the wrongs of slavery. Many people listened to what abolitionists had to say about the issue of slavery.*

war officially ended, he became one of the first members of the Pennsylvania Abolition Society, a group of people who wanted to free America's black slaves. When Eliza was 10 years old, her mother died, too, and she was sent to Richmond to live with her uncle.

On January 10, 1818, John and Eliza were married at St. John's Episcopal Church on Church Hill in Richmond. In October, they had their first child, Elizabeth. They would eventually have two more children, Anna and John. Although Elizabeth's parents had not been born and raised in the South, they became prominent in the upper class of Richmond society. Eliza was a refined, gracious woman, which was typical of most Southern ladies. John's hardware store soon expanded to five very successful businesses, and the Van Lews were able to enjoy wealth and a high social position.

The Van Lews' three-story house was magnificent, often called a mansion by the townspeople. It was situated on Church Hill, the highest of Richmond's seven hills, in an area that only the wealthy could afford. The house and elaborate gardens were huge, covering an entire city block. Large white pillars towered to the top edge of the expansive front porch. From her house, Elizabeth had a

Elizabeth Van Lew's parents were married at St. John's Episcopal Church in Richmond.

clear view of the city and the James River below. At the bottom of the hill, not far from the mansion, was the family's farm, where about a dozen of their slaves planted and harvested crops. Owning slaves was a common practice at that time, especially in the South.

The Van Lew mansion, built in 1802, was located at 2311 E. Grace St. in Richmond, Virginia.

Inside her beautiful house, Elizabeth especially

enjoyed the family's large personal library. Learning was very important to the Van Lews, and every year they set aside $50 to buy books. Her father encouraged reading and learning, and often talked with his children about what was going on in the country. Elizabeth learned to understand politics and form her own opinions about important issues of the day.

The Van Lew children also had the advantage of music, dancing lessons, and tutors that came to the house to help them with their studies. When the children got older, they were sent to the best, most expensive private schools. In the early 1830s, when Elizabeth was a young teenager, her parents sent her to Philadelphia, her mother's childhood home, to attend a prominent girl's school. There she lived with one of her mother's relatives in a city that was more than 10 times larger than Richmond. She learned a lot at school and in the bustling city, which was full of things to see and new ideas to ponder.

One thing Elizabeth thought about was slavery. At school, one of her teachers was strongly opposed to people owning other people as slaves. There were also abolitionist groups forming in Philadelphia that wanted to put an end to slavery in the entire country. The idea was dividing Americans. Some thought no one should own another human being, while others felt slavery was a necessary part of the economy.

A slave named Henry "Box" Brown was shipped in a box from Richmond, Virginia, to his freedom in Philadelphia, Pennsylvania, in 1849.

When Elizabeth completed her education, she returned to Richmond with strong antislavery views that would establish the course of the rest of her life.

Elizabeth and her father did not agree on the issue of slavery. She often begged him to give the family slaves their freedom, but he always refused.

In 1843, when Elizabeth was 25 years old, her father died. In his will, he gave each of his three children $10,000 and his wife the rest of his money,

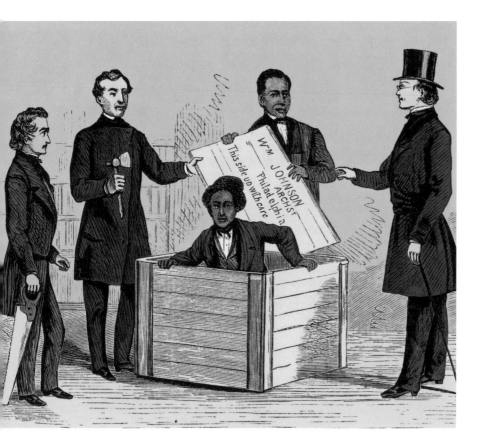

property, and belongings. But he clearly stated that his wife could not sell the slaves or set them free. She only had the right to use them. The will went on to say that when his wife died, his property and his slaves were to be divided equally among his three children.

Elizabeth had lost the battle with her father over the issue of slavery, even after his death. She still was not able to legally set their slaves free. But she would not stop trying. ॐ

3 SET THE SLAVES FREE

⸜⸝⸜⸝

A few months after the death of John Van Lew in 1843, Elizabeth's sister Anna married Dr. Joseph Klapp and moved to Philadelphia. Her brother John began managing their father's hardware businesses. Elizabeth lived at home with her mother. They often took part in Richmond's high society, holding lavish balls and receptions in their house and hosting elaborate garden parties. From time to time, they would travel in their horse-drawn coach to White Sulphur Springs, one of the finest resorts of their day.

Many well-known people were guests at the Van Lew mansion, including John Marshall, chief justice of the Supreme Court, and John Adams, who had served as the second president of the United States. Famous singer, Jenny Lind, once sang in the Van

Slaves were transported south from Richmond, Virginia, after a slave sale in about 1850.

Lews' living room; Edgar Allan Poe read his famous poem "The Raven" there.

One guest that had a great impact on Elizabeth was Fredrika Bremer from Sweden, who visited the Van Lew mansion in June 1851. She was on a trip across the United States to meet its important women. As a strong opponent of slavery, Bremer also wanted to see what she considered to be the shameful practice of slavery in the United States.

Fredrika Bremer (1801-1865), Swedish novelist and abolitionist

Van Lew was glad to show her what slavery was like and drove her around Richmond to see it first-hand. A large tobacco manufacturing company was one of their stops. When they arrived, about 100 slaves were working with tobacco in large rooms.

The slaves sang while they worked, sometimes as a large chorus and other times in small groups. The songs were often made up as they sang, sometimes telling about their joys but more often about their sorrows.

Although Bremer admired their singing, she was saddened by their plight. Van Lew was also very moved by their condition and could not keep from crying. Bremer later wrote:

> *If these slaves had only any future, any thing to hope for, to strive for, to live for, any prospect before them, then I should not deplore their lot—but nothing, nothing!!!*

It wasn't long before Van Lew figured out a way around her father's will in order to free their slaves. Since she could not legally set them free, she found a way to unofficially allow them to live as free people. She just told them they could leave.

Perhaps there was some kind of private, unofficial agreement with them that they were free to go. However, since a Virginia law stated that newly freed slaves must leave the state within one year,

Slaves rolling tobacco packed in barrels to market in Virginia

their freedom was kept a secret, and many of them stayed with the family as hired workers.

Throughout the 1850s, the conflict over slavery grew more intense. New states were being added to the United States, and heated arguments arose over the issue of slavery. Should new states be added as free states or slave states? Northerners thought new states should be free, while Southerners wanted slavery permitted. Some thought each state should decide for itself, and others thought slavery should be abolished completely. The people in the South claimed their farms and economy would fail if they could not own slaves. The division between the

North and the South widened.

Van Lew held firm to her views against slavery, which was not a popular position to take in a Southern state like Virginia. In 1859, people were talking a lot about slavery, politics, and the upcoming presidential election. Van Lew liked Abraham Lincoln, the candidate for the new Republican Party, but her friends and neighbors did not.

Lincoln and his party were against new states coming in as slave states, although they agreed the South still had the right to own slaves. Even so, most Southerners didn't want Lincoln elected as president. They threatened to secede, or pull out of the United States, if he was elected.

Van Lew wrote in her journal about what the people of Virginia were saying:

Abraham Lincoln (1809-1865)

People were, if anything, more morbid than ever on the subject of slavery, and I heard a member of the Virginia Legislature say

*that anyone speaking against it [slavery],
or doubting its divinity, ought to be hung.
... Another gentleman, a state senator, told
me that members of the senate did not dare
to speak as they thought and felt, that they
were afraid.*

Lincoln won the 1860 election and became the 16th president of the United States. Some Southern states followed through on their threat to secede, and on December 20, 1860, South Carolina became the first state to officially break way from the Union.

Jefferson Davis (1808-1889), president of the Confederate States of America

By February 1861, six other Southern states—Mississippi, Florida, Alabama, Georgia, Louisiana, and Texas—had joined South Carolina. Then they decided to form their own country—the Confederate States of America. They chose Jefferson Davis, a senator from Mississippi, as president of the Confederate States. Soon, Virginia, Arkansas, Tennessee, and North Carolina also pulled out of the United States and joined the Confederacy—11 states in all.

Davis wanted to buy all the federal land and military forts located within the Confederate states. Lincoln said the Confederate states were not an official country and refused his request. But Davis would not be stopped. On April 10, 1861, he demanded that Fort Sumter in Charleston, South Carolina, be given to the Confederacy. Federal soldiers stationed at the fort refused to surrender. On April 12, 1861, at 4:30 A.M., 4,000 Confederates under the leadership of General P.G.T. Beauregard opened fire with 50 cannons.

Within 35 hours, Union troops surrendered to the South. The Confederates, or rebels, as they were called, raised the Confederate flag with its stars and bars in triumph above Fort Sumter. The American Civil War had begun, and Elizabeth Van Lew found herself suddenly living within the borders of a new country—a country founded on beliefs she strongly opposed. ❧

Fort Sumter was built to protect Charleston Harbor along the Atlantic Coast of the United States. Construction began in 1829 on a man-made island made of sea shells and granite rock brought in from northern quarries. The fort was a pentagonal structure that stood 50 feet (150 meters) high and had walls 8-12 feet (240-360 centimeters) thick.

4 PRISON MESSENGER

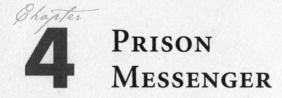

Elizabeth Van Lew disagreed with the principles of the Confederacy in two areas. The new government supported slavery; she did not. The Southern states encouraged other states to break away from the Union; she believed strongly that the states should stay together. Neighbors and friends began to shun and even threaten Elizabeth and her mother. It was difficult to be a Unionist in a Confederate state. She confided to her journal:

> *The threats, the scowls, the frowns of an infuriated community; who can write of them? I have had brave men shake their fingers in my face and say terrible things. We had threats of being driven away, threats of fire, and threats of death.*

The Confederate flag had 11 stars, which stood for the 11 states that seceded from the Union.

... I was a silent and sorrowful spectator of the rise and spread of the secession mania.

In May 1861, the new Confederate government voted to move the new country's capital from Montgomery, Alabama, to Richmond, Virginia. High over the state Capitol in Richmond now flew the Confederate flag.

Opinions were strongly divided in all parts of the North and the South. Violence erupted in Baltimore, Maryland, when people in favor of seceding from the Union attacked Northern soldiers on their way to Washington, D.C. Citizens of Richmond celebrated the attack by marching through town with torches. Elizabeth watched the victory celebration from her garden and fell to her knees and prayed a verse from the Bible, "Father, forgive them, for they know not what they do."

Elizabeth wrote in her journal, "Surely madness was upon the people." She quietly decided she would do whatever she could to see the South defeated and the states restored as one country. She was also determined to use her time and money to set slaves free and work to put an end to this horrible practice that kept people in bondage.

As the people of Richmond prepared for war, the city was abuzz with politicians and Southern soldiers. Confederate Army volunteers arrived by train, and soon regiments of about 1,000 troops each were organized. Richmond women busied themselves making bandages and turning rooms and buildings into medical facilities.

They organized sewing groups to hastily make uniforms for thousands of their Confederate soldiers. When Elizabeth and her mother were asked to help make shirts, they politely refused. After being

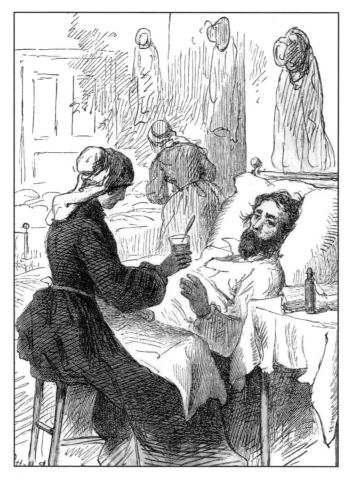

A woman nurse treats a wounded soldier in a Civil War hospital. Before the Civil War, most nurses were men.

criticized and threatened for not helping, they reluctantly offered to deliver religious books to Confederate soldiers encamped around the city.

In July 1861, just three months after the Battle of Fort Sumter, another battle broke out near the town of Manassas, Virginia. About 4,700 soldiers died in the Battle of Bull Run, as it was called. It was the bloodiest battle yet on American soil. Thousands were wounded on each side, and more than 1,000 injured soldiers sought medical treatment in Richmond. The number of wounded was so great that homes had to become makeshift hospitals, and nearly every woman tended to the injured in some way. Although the Union was defeated at that battle and retreated on July 21, both sides had paid a dear price—thousands of casualties.

The Confederates captured many Northern soldiers in the battle, and now they had to decide what to do with them. So many prisoners were streaming into Richmond that factories and warehouses throughout the city had to be quickly turned into prisons. But they needed a more permanent place for the prisoners. Several months later, in March 1862, Luther Libby, a Richmond businessman, was given just 48 hours to leave the three buildings he owned at Cary and Dock streets on the west side of the city. The four-story buildings were taken in such haste that Libby's sign remained in front, and thus,

Libby Prison
at Richmond,
Virginia

the prison came to be called Libby Prison.

On the first floor, rooms were turned into offices for the guards, and a kitchen was set up. Prisoners were kept on the second through fourth floors; the basement was reserved for the most dangerous soldiers, the spies, and the slaves who were sentenced to death. Libby Prison could hold about 1,200 prisoners comfortably, but usually, many more were crammed into the buildings.

That same month, Union forces began preparing for another battle. Union General George B. McClellan assembled more than 10,000 soldiers at Fort Monroe in Hampton, Virginia, to prepare to fight their way west to Richmond. By May, Union soldiers were on the outskirts of Richmond, and on

May 31, fierce fighting broke out. Confederate General Joseph E. Johnston was severely wounded and replaced by General Robert E. Lee. McClellan continued to push his way toward Richmond.

Elizabeth Van Lew and her mother were hoping that McClellan and his soldiers would soon enter Richmond in victory. They even prepared a room in their mansion where McClellan could stay, once he got to Richmond. Three weeks later, McClellan still had not entered the city. On June 20, Elizabeth wrote in her journal, "How long is this to last? We are in hourly expectation of a battle."

Five days later, on June 25, 1862, the Seven Days' Battles began a few miles east of Richmond. As the fighting moved toward the city, citizens watched from their rooftops. On June 26, Van Lew and her friend, Eliza Carrington, rode toward the battles on their way to visit their friends, the Botts. That evening, Van Lew wrote in her journal:

> *We found Mr. Botts and family listening to the roar of the artillery. The windows rattled. The flash of the bursting shells could be seen. ... About nine o'clock it ceased and with a kind good night we left our friends; returned by another road; reached home about ten; found the family much excited, the fight having approached so near our house that the bursting of the shells could be distinctly*

seen from the home window, and the house shook with each report.

More than 36,000 soldiers died on both sides in those battles. The Union was forced to retreat. Thousands of wounded Northern soldiers filled Richmond's hospitals and homes that served as medical centers. Union troops were captured by the thousands and brought to the city's already crowded prisons, bringing the number of prisoners in Richmond to 8,000.

Elizabeth had heard about Libby Prison, which was just six blocks from the Van Lew mansion at the

Citizens tend to the wounded in the streets of Richmond, Virginia, after an 1862 Civil War battle.

base of Church Hill. Prisoners were also in ware-houses and at Belle Isle, a man-made island in the James River. Conditions in the prisons were terrible and got worse as more and more prisoners were brought in. Food was scarce, and the food they had was often not good enough to eat. Conditions were especially bad at Belle Isle. The bread was full of bugs, and meals included crumbled corncobs. Three hundred prisoners would eventually die at Belle Isle during the Civil War.

Van Lew was deeply dismayed at the stories she heard of abuse and mistreatment of Union prison-ers. Determined to help them in any way she could, Elizabeth went to see Lieutenant David H. Todd, commander of Libby Prison. She asked to be a prison nurse, but Todd refused. After all, he said, the prisoners didn't deserve the care of a nice Southern lady. That didn't stop her, though, and she contacted someone above Todd—Confederate secretary of the treasury, Christopher G. Memminger. He, too, claimed that Northern prisoners were not worthy of her kind attention. She was not discouraged, how-ever, and reminded him of what he once said at a religious meeting: "If we wish 'our cause' to suc-ceed, we must begin with charity to the thankless." It was enough to make Memminger think, and he gave Van Lew permission to see Confederate Brigadier John Henry Winder.

With a letter of introduction from Memminger, Van Lew went to her appointment with Winder. Knowing he was somewhat conceited, she resorted to flattery and complimented his silver hair before making her request. Her charm must have worked, because she left his office with a note that gave her permission to visit Libby Prison. Although she could not go inside the prison, she could bring food, books, and gifts to the prisoners.

Thus began Elizabeth Van Lew's charitable prison work, but it was much more than that. On her frequent visits, she brought Todd gifts of buttermilk and gingerbread, so he would not hesitate to deliver her gifts to the inmates. This gentle Southern lady with her arms full of food and books was a welcome sight at Libby Prison.

The guards looked forward to her visits and her gifts of money that she used as bribes to persuade them to do what she wanted. With her charm and her money, she soon had a lot of control over the guards. She received regular reports from them on the

Lieutenant David H. Todd, commander of Libby Prison in Richmond, was the half-brother of Mary Todd Lincoln, wife of Abraham Lincoln and first lady of the United States. Todd was known for his brutal treatment of prisoners, and once he even said he wanted to shoot his brother-in-law, Abraham Lincoln. At the end of 1861, he was sent to fight in the war. He died from wounds he received at the Battle of Vicksburg, Mississippi, in 1863.

condition of the prisoners and made sure they got what they needed—additional food, clothing, bedding, or fresh air. Often, she convinced Confederate doctors at the prison to send Union soldiers to a hospital. Then she could visit them in person and sometimes help them plan their escapes. One Union officer told about her hospital visits and how "our officers and men felt the effects of her care ... she alone went from cot to cot where lay a sufferer in blue."

Usually, the gifts she brought to the prison contained much more than just food or reading materials. Inside were secret messages, letters, and money from home. She also included nice little notes with

Painting by Libby prisoner Major Otto Botticke shows prison life inside Libby Prison in 1862.

encouraging words. Often the words had hidden meanings, which the prisoners soon figured out. The books she loaned them had coded messages inside. Sometimes words here and there were lightly underlined. With a little piecing together, prisoners made sentences out of them—sentences with important information and questions about the war.

Since Van Lew wanted the books returned, the prisoners learned to put hidden messages and answers to her questions in them. Sometimes, they poked tiny holes under letters or words, which could be seen when held up to the light. The letters and words were put together to make a message about what the prisoners had heard or seen.

Anything they could pass on to Van Lew was important, and she would immediately mail the information to Union generals.

Van Lew smuggled documents into the prison by concealing them in her gifts of food. She often used an old French-style metal plate with a double bottom. Hot water was supposed to be poured into the space between the two bottoms to keep food warm on top, but Van Lew used the space to smuggle documents. One guard got suspicious of her double-bottomed plate, however, so she brought it one day filled with boiling water. She wrapped the plate carefully with her shawl to protect her hands from the heat, and when the guard questioned her, she unwrapped it and quickly placed it in his hands for inspection. After burning his hands on the hot metal, he never again questioned her about the plate.

Now and then, prison authorities refused to let Van Lew make her deliveries. But she would go back to General Winder and get back her privileges to visit the prisons and hospitals. Most of the time, she kept a good relationship with prison authorities through flattery, charm, and gifts. She often distracted them by mumbling meaninglessly or singing softly. The guards just laughed at her, but her act must have been convincing, because they tended to ignore her.

To the people of Richmond, Van Lew was once a

respectable Southern woman. But now they resented her anti-Confederate views and activities. People made threatening remarks to her and shook their fingers in her face to shame her for helping the Union. They threatened to drive her out of town, burn her house, and even kill her.

The Moore Hospital on Main Street in Richmond, Virginia, was one of several medical facilities where wounded soldiers were treated during the Civil War.

Local newspapers began criticizing and insulting Elizabeth and her mother for paying attention to Union soldiers and spending money to help the Yankees, as Northerners were called. An article in the July 29, 1861, *Richmond Enquirer* read:

> *Two ladies, a mother and a daughter, living on Church Hill, have lately attracted*

*public notice by their assiduous atten-
tions to the Yankee prisoners ... these two
women have been expending their opulent
[wealthy] means in aiding and giving
comfort to the miscreants [criminals]
who have invaded our sacred soil.*

The *Richmond Dispatch* then published an article that called the women Yankee offshoots and warned them to be careful, or they would be "exposed and dealt with as alien enemies to the country." In spite of the threats, the Van Lews continued to support the prisoners and the Union.

As the war became more intense, the people of Richmond grew to hate Van Lew even more and called her names like "Crazy Bet." She used it to her advantage, however, and acted in even more peculiar ways. She muttered strange words to herself as she walked along the streets and learned to have a somewhat confused look on her face. She started dressing in tattered clothing and took on an untidy appearance. She sported strange hats and swung her basket to and fro. After all, she had to do whatever she could to protect herself and her mother from Confederate revenge. How long would her fellow Southerners put up with her pro-Northern deeds?

When both sides started inspecting mail sent across enemy lines, it became too dangerous for Van Lew to mail documents and information. Now she

resorted to personal deliveries. However, she could not do it all on her own. There were too many deliveries for one person, and she was too well-known for her support of the Union. She would easily be suspected of underground work. So she started using friends, slaves, and freed slaves in the Richmond area to carry messages across Confederate lines. Thus began Van Lew's spy organization, the Richmond Union Underground. It would be instrumental in the North winning the Civil War. ✍

A tent served as a temporary post office for the Union Army during the Civil war.

5 SPY NETWORK

❧❧❧

One of the most valuable agents in Elizabeth Van Lew's spy network was Mary Elizabeth Bowser. In fact, she was one of the Van Lews' slaves. Several years before the war began, Van Lew allowed her to leave the mansion. Bowser went to Philadelphia, Pennsylvania, where she attended school. But now, Van Lew needed this intelligent, educated woman back in Richmond. She had a plan, and a black woman would best be able to carry it out.

Van Lew needed a spy in the Confederate White House, where Jefferson Davis lived with his family and where many Confederate meetings were held. Bowser was able to get a job there and began serving Davis his meals in the dining room and cleaning up around the house. When he met there with his military staff, she often overheard their conversations. She was allowed to go about freely in any part of the house, including Davis' private study, where she read war communications and other documents. It was unusual for a slave to be able to read at that time, so Davis didn't suspect Bowser of any wrongdoing. He didn't bother to conceal papers or plans when she was in the room.

Undercover Union spy, Mary Bowser, looks over the shoulder of Confederate President Jefferson Davis to read secret military documents.

Mary Bowser had a remarkable talent—a photographic memory—that enabled her to remember and recite what she read, word for word. On a regular basis, often in the middle of the night, Bowser sneaked out of Davis' house and quietly made her way to the Van Lew farm. There she met Van Lew or one of the other agents to relay the information she had gathered in her head. Sometimes Bowser passed information to Thomas McNiven, a member of another network of Union spies, who used a Richmond bakery as a cover for his spy operations. He often delivered fresh bread to the Confederate White House, making it easy for Bowser to give him information.

It was important for spies to know if someone was another spy or an enemy. Union spies often wore carved peach seeds in the shape of a three-leafed clover to identify each other. When the clover was turned right side up, it was not safe to talk to each other. When it was upside down, spies could safely communicate.

Another Van Lew spy, Erasmus Ross, was an undercover agent inside Libby Prison. He worked as a guard, checking to make sure inmates were present at daily roll calls. Ross was a clever pretender. He acted mean and nasty so Confederate guards wouldn't suspect him. Even the prisoners didn't have any idea he was on their side and considered him one of the most

The South also had many women spies during the Civil War. Belle Boyd was just 18 years old when she began delivering information about the Union Army to the Confederacy. Rose O'Neal Greenhow used her important status in Washington, D.C., to collect information about the Union and pass it along to Confederate leaders.

cruel of all the guards. But Ross helped many prisoners escape from the horrible conditions of Libby Prison. Union Captain William H. Lounsbery was one of the lucky ones who got away, thanks to Ross.

One day after roll call, Ross gruffly ordered Lounsbery to go his office, where he then ordered him to go to the kitchen. When Lounsbery arrived at the prison kitchen, he saw a Confederate Army uniform hanging on the back of a chair. Without hesitation, he put on the uniform, walked freely out of the prison, and stepped out onto the street. He had only taken a few steps when a black man stopped him and asked if he wanted to go to Elizabeth Van Lew's house. One escapee later recalled:

> *Miss Van Lew kept two or three bright, sharp colored men on the watch near Libby prison, who were always ready to conduct an escaped prisoner to a place of safety. Not all of them were secreted at her house—for there were several safe places of refuge in Richmond supported by her means.*

The man showed Lounsbery the way to the Van Lew mansion, where he stayed in a secret attic room until he could safely travel to the North. During the war, Van Lew hid many Union soldiers in this secret room with its slanted floor and sloping ceiling. The small door in the wall was just big enough for someone to go through, and it fastened only on the inside.

Van Lew figured out many ways for prisoners and information to get from her house to the North. Her agents transported people and documents without raising suspicion or getting caught by using five stations, or stops, along the way. The first station, of course, was the Van Lew mansion. From there, they went the short distance to the Van Lew farm. Three more places finally brought them to safety.

Some of her spies carried information in large food baskets, often filled with eggs. One egg was

As many as 50 to 60 men could be hidden in the secret room on the top floor of the Van Lew mansion.

usually just an empty shell, filled with a tiny piece of paper, and then carefully pieced back together. Some spies dressed like seamstresses and hid documents, medical supplies, and food in their sewing baskets. The women's full skirts and wired hoops that held them out were also perfect hiding places for messages, medicine, food, and money.

Messages were often written in a cipher, or code, where each letter of the alphabet stood for another letter. At times, Van Lew and her spies wrote a regular friendly letter, but between the lines was a secret message written with invisible ink. To make the ink appear, Union officers simply had to put milk on the paper, and the ink turned black so they could read it.

Transporting people, documents, and messages was dangerous, no matter how careful the spies were. Some spies weren't as fortunate as Van Lew's network and were arrested for their undercover work. Actress and Union spy, Pauline Cushman, was arrested by the Confederates and sentenced to death. But before she could be executed, the Union Army rescued her. On every journey, spies ran the risk of being caught and possibly put to death.

Van Lew lived under constant suspicion and did what she could to protect herself. She usually stayed in the good graces of the Confederates and was careful to make important relationships. One of her connections was with the man who replaced David H.

Todd as the new head of Libby Prison—Captain George C. Gibbs. Before he moved to Richmond, Van Lew offered Gibbs and his family a place to live in her house. He accepted her kind hospitality and moved in to her mansion. What a clever way to keep up on what was happening at Libby Prison! ✍

6 THE GREAT ESCAPE

Chapter

❧❦❧

Libby Prison was an active place, usually over-crowded with Union prisoners and often filled with news of escapes. Usually, Elizabeth Van Lew was somehow involved in those prison breaks. In December 1863, two men escaped from the prison hospital and hid for 10 days at a farm on the outer edge of Richmond. One of Van Lew's closest connections in her network, William S. Rowley, was the owner of the farm.

One of the escapees, Captain Harry S. Howard, was able to sneak out of Richmond and go to Washington, D.C. He reported directly to Union General Benjamin F. Butler that Van Lew and Rowley were good sources of information in the South. Butler sent Howard back to Rowley's farm to

Escaped prisoners from Libby Prison were helped by Union soldiers.

sign up Van Lew and Rowley as official federal agents who would work directly for the government of the United States. Van Lew accepted the position and officially became a federal agent.

Meanwhile, the prisoners at Libby were hard at work digging an escape route. Two Union prisoners, Colonel Thomas E. Rose and Major Andrew G. Hamilton, were responsible for the escape plan at Libby. They studied the layout of the prison and drew up a plan—an underground tunnel. With the help of other prisoners, they started by cutting through the back of a large fireplace in the kitchen. After about two weeks, they broke through the wall and cut down to a rat-infested storage room in the basement. Then the men began digging a tunnel they hoped would provide their passage to freedom.

Their first three attempts failed—the first tunnel flooded, the second collapsed, and the third couldn't be finished because something was blocking it. But Rose and Hamilton refused to give up. In January, they sent word to Van Lew that they were planning an escape. They would need someplace to hide, if they were successful.

Soon they started their fourth attempt at a tunnel, and this time they were successful. About five men worked day and night in shifts, digging underground and hauling out dirt that they hid under piles of straw in the prison basement. The men who

The fireplace in the Libby Prison kitchen, where prisoners started digging their escape tunnel

weren't digging had to distract the guards and make them believe no one was missing. Whenever Ross took roll call, some of the prisoners would run to the end of the line after they had been counted, so they could be counted again. That way, it seemed like all the prisoners were present. They thought they were fooling Ross, but he actually knew what they were doing, looked the other way, and ignored their tricks. After all, he was part of the Union underground, a spy for the North.

Late on the night of February 8, 1864, the tunnel

was completed. It wove underground about 50 to 60 feet (150 to 180 meters) under a vacant piece of land next to the prison and ended up under a tobacco shed on the other side of the street. The next night, February 9, the prisoners distracted the guards with music and dancing, and one by one, they started slipping through the hole in the back of the kitchen fireplace. They squeezed through the tunnel that was only 2 feet (60 centimeters) across and less than 2 feet (60 cm) high. It was cold, dark, and full of rats, but the men were determined to crawl their way to freedom. By morning, there were 109 prisoners who didn't show up for roll call. They were somewhere in Richmond, and Libby officials were shocked and enraged.

Van Lew had also been making plans for their escape, getting her house ready to hide the runaway prisoners. She wrote in her journal:

> We knew there was to be an exit, had been told to prepare, & had one of our parlors or rather end rooms—had dark blankets nailed up at the windows & gas had been kept burning in it ... for about 3 weeks. We were so ready for them, beds prepared in there.

But Elizabeth didn't know the exact day the prisoners would attempt to escape. On February 9, she wasn't home. She was with her brother John, who

Drawing shows the escape tunnel from Libby Prison to the tobacco shed on the other side of the street.

had been serving against his will in the Confederate Army. Now he had deserted and was hiding out in the home of a pro-Union family. Elizabeth, disguised as a farmwoman with a sunbonnet on her head and a basket on her arm, set out to meet him. She planned to help him get across Confederate lines and travel safely to the North. The next day, Elizabeth heard about the escape from Libby Prison:

> *In the morning our driver came out with a basket full of supplies. As soon as he called, he said that there was great trouble & excitement ... that many prisoners had escaped during the night; and that some had come to his door ... & begged to come in.*

She hurried home, very upset that she had not been there to let the prisoners into her home. Some of the escapees had asked her servants to let them in, but had been turned away because the servants were not sure who they were. Some of the men found refuge, but 48 prisoners were recaptured, and two died. Rose, the mastermind of the operation, was one of the unfortunate ones who had to return to Libby. Confederate officials took steps to make sure no other prisoners would escape. They placed barrels of gunpowder around the prison and warned that if anyone attempted another breakout, the place would be blown up. Meanwhile, Elizabeth started working to get the remaining 59 escapees out of the South.

Other prisoners also needed Van Lew's help. More than 11,000 were still in Libby and Belle Isle, where the men were especially in desperate need. At the end of February 1864, Van Lew got permission to visit the outskirts of Belle Isle. What she saw was horrifying:

> *The long lines of forsaken, despairing, hopeless-looking beings, who, within this hollow square, looked upon us, gaunt hunger staring from their sunken eyes. ... men lying on the ground, some without a thing over or under them ... within a few, very few steps ... the newly made graves of their late companions.*

The men were dying at a rate of up to 10 a day. During the winter of 1863-1864, hundreds of prisoners died. By that time, the war had been raging for

Many prisoners at Belle Isle froze or starved to death during the Civil War.

almost three years, and the Confederacy was short on supplies. It couldn't feed and care for all these prisoners, but they couldn't let them go, either. So the men continued to die at a shocking rate.

The Confederates began moving prisoners to Georgia. Van Lew sent a letter to Butler to let him know what they were doing. It was perhaps one of the most important messages she sent him. It helped the Union prepare for a raid on Richmond.

Her letter told Butler how many Confederate soldiers were busy moving prisoners and were often out of town. The messenger who delivered the letter passed on Van Lew's advice that "Richmond could be taken easier now than at any other time since the war began."

Butler immediately sent Van Lew's letter and a record of his conversation with the messenger to Edwin M. Stanton, the secretary of war for the Union. Stanton took the information directly to President Lincoln, who gave orders for a raid on Richmond. It was to be led by Brigadier General Judson Kilpatrick and young Colonel Ulric Dahlgren.

Dahlgren was known for his courage, although at times he was a reckless soldier. He had lost his right leg at the Battle of Gettysburg, but he was still able to lead his soldiers with the help of a wooden leg. Back in full action, he saw this assignment as his chance for glory.

Nineteen days after the Libby Prison escape, Kilpatrick and Dahlgren set out with Union troops from their camp about 50 miles (80 km) north of Richmond. Dahlgren and his unit of 460 men would approach Richmond from the west. His plan was to free the prisoners at Belle Isle and then those held in warehouses throughout the city. In the meantime, Kilpatrick and about 3,000 soldiers prepared to attack from the north.

On March 1, 1864, alarms sounded in Richmond. The Union was at the northern edge of the city. Meanwhile, Dahlgren and his soldiers couldn't get across the deep waters of the James River and

headed east to look for another route. A group of Richmond citizens called the home guard went out to block them. The group was made up of anyone who was not already fighting the war, such as factory workers, old men, young boys, politicians, and wounded soldiers. But they fought fiercely, and although Dahlgren got within two miles (3.2 km) of Richmond, he was forced to retreat. The next day, March 2, Dahlgren and his men walked into a trap—the Confederate cavalry had gotten in front of them and ambushed them at 11:30 P.M. Dahlgren was killed, shot five times, and many of his soldiers were captured and taken to prison.

Confederate soldiers took everything that was

Union Brigadier General Judson Kilpatrick leads his cavalry to raid Richmond, Virginia, and rescue Union prisoners.

valuable from Dahlgren's body, including his wooden leg. There by the side of the road, they buried him in a shallow, muddy hole. Five days later, on March 6, Confederate soldiers came back, dug up his body, and paraded it triumphantly through Richmond in a pine coffin. Large crowds gathered to see it and celebrate a Confederate victory. Some threw rocks at the coffin as the soldiers marched through the city. Then by direct order of President Davis, they buried Dahlgren in a secret location in the early hours of the morning.

Van Lew's spies soon set out to search for Dahlgren's body. They finally found a witness to the secret burial. An old black cemetery worker at Oakwood Cemetery in Richmond had seen it all. As he hid behind a tree, he had watched the Confederates bury Dahlgren in a shallow, unmarked grave. After they left, he marked the grave so he could find it again.

Frederick W.E. Lohmann ran a grocery store in Richmond, Virginia, but he also was a spy for the Union during the Civil War. Lohmann and his friend, Christian Burging, secretly took many pro-Union citizens out of the South by bringing them to the Rapahanock and Potomac rivers so they could cross over to the North.

Early on a dark morning in April 1864, Van Lew's agents—Frederick Lohmann, John Lohmann, and Martin Lipscomb—went to Oakwood Cemetery and persuaded the cemetery worker to show them Dahlgren's grave. They dug up the body and took it to William

Rowley's farm, where they waited for the arrival of their leader, Elizabeth Van Lew.

When she arrived, Van Lew held a unique type of funeral service, cutting off several locks of Dahlgren's hair to send to the young soldier's father. In her journal, she wrote that "every true Union heart who knew of this day's work, felt happier for having charge of this precious dust [Dahlgren's body]."

A picture of Union Colonel Ulric Dahlgren appeared in Harper's Weekly *on March 26, 1864.*

The first four months of 1864 had been difficult for the North and the South. But the rest of the year would be worse, and one side would suffer defeat. ✍

7 THE FALL OF RICHMOND

❧⟨✦⟩❧

As 1864 moved on, Elizabeth Van Lew became more careful. She wrote in her journal, "I always went to bed at night with anything dangerous on paper beside me so as to be able to destroy it in a moment." Living in Richmond was dangerous, and she met cautiously with other Union supporters:

> When the cold wind would blow in the darkest & stormiest night, Union people would visit one another. With shutters closed & curtains pinned together, how have we been startled at the barking of a dog and drawn nearer together, the pallor [paleness] coming over our faces & the blood rushing to our hearts.

Southern forces were getting weary of war, their

Union General Ulysses S. Grant leads the charge at the Battle of the Wilderness, May 5-7, 1864.

supplies were scarce, and they were no longer confident that the North could be defeated. Although they didn't give up hope, they were in a state of despair. The severe winter had caused a shortage of food, and people were starving. Elizabeth recalled that "women are begging for bread with tears in their eyes." Richmond prisoners were also suffering—from cold, starvation, and disease.

In March, President Lincoln appointed Grant commander of the entire Union Army. Grant planned attacks all over the South to defeat the Confederates and end the war. One of his targets was Richmond. Again and again, he tried to sweep around General Lee's forces, but Lee blocked him every time. In the meantime, General Butler was on

City Point on the James River was one of Union General Ulysses S. Grant's headquarters.

his way up the James River toward Richmond from the south. On the battlefield that came to be called the Wilderness, the flash of guns set trees on fire. Many soldiers burned to death where they lay wounded. On May 14, 1864, the fighting was so close to Van Lew's house that she wrote, "Awakened by the cannon. ... The firing has been uninterrupted all day, and so loud as to jar the windows."

For six weeks, fighting continued without a break, and Grant repeatedly attacked the rebels, who refused to give up. In June, the Union needed Van Lew's help. Colonel George H. Sharpe, chief of intelligence, made contact with her right after he arrived at Grant's headquarters at City Point, Virginia, just 20 miles (32 km) from Richmond.

Sharpe needed Van Lew to gather information in Richmond and bring it to Grant at headquarters. She quickly rallied her network of spies to carry messages to Union scouts placed at five relay stations between Richmond and City Point.

While battles raged for the next several months, Van Lew's network took military information and personal messages from family and friends to the soldiers at City Point. One spy, Sylvanus J. Brown, even carried people out of Richmond and helped them escape to the Union. No one suspected him of hauling anything other than produce in his cart.

The Confederates were watching Van Lew's house more carefully now. In September, the Van Lews were formally investigated, and their friends and neighbors were questioned. Since Elizabeth's mother was the head of the household, she became the main target of the investigation. Elizabeth worried about her mother's safety and hoped their social status would protect them from any charges.

There was a shortage of horses to use in battle, and soldiers even came looking for Van Lew's horse. When she heard they were coming, she quickly prepared an upper room of her house with a bed of straw and carefully led her horse up the stairs. When the soldiers arrived, they never checked an unlikely place like a bedroom for her horse.

By New Year's Day, 1865, the atmosphere in

Richmond was one of hopelessness. Constant rain turned the streets to mud, businesses were closed down, and Confederate money was nearly worthless. Food was scarce, and people were begging on the streets. Elizabeth wrote to Grant, "May God

Most of the Civil War battles were fought in Southern states.

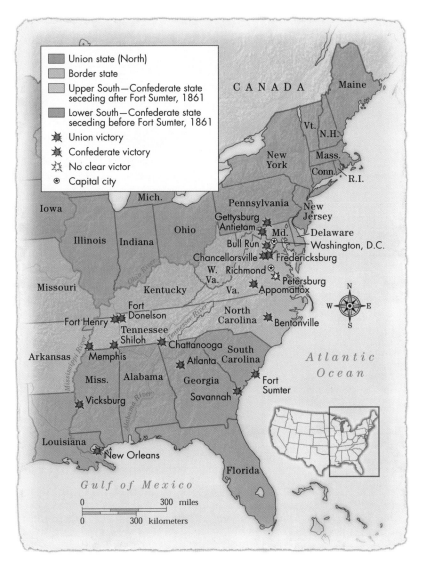

Map legend: Union state (North); Border state; Upper South—Confederate state seceding after Fort Sumter, 1861; Lower South—Confederate state seceding before Fort Sumter, 1861; Union victory; Confederate victory; No clear victor; Capital city.

bless and bring you soon to deliver us. We are all in an awful situation here. There is great want of food."

Large portions of the South were now under Union control, and Union General William T. Sherman was on his way to help. Van Lew's agents were very active, traveling almost constantly between Richmond and City Point. Colonel David B. Parker, one of Grant's staff members, later told about one method the spies used to transport information:

Every day two of her trusty negro servants drove into Richmond with something to sell—milk, chickens, garden-truck, etc. These negroes wore great, strong brogans [shoes], with soles of immense thickness, made by a Richmond shoemaker. ... The soles of these shoes were double and hollow, and in them were carried through the lines letters, maps, plans, etc., which were regularly delivered to General Grant at City Point the next morning.

When Richmond was set on fire, Confederate President Jefferson Davis fled. On May 10, 1865, federal soldiers captured him at Irwinville, Georgia. From 1865 to 1867 he was imprisoned at Fortress Monroe, Virginia. Davis was charged with treason in 1866 but was released the next year on a $100,000 bond. In 1868 the federal government dropped the case against him.

It was dangerous for Van Lew's spies. Several of them were arrested for helping people escape to the North. Some were released for lack of evidence or perhaps due to a good-sized bribe or two, and others were put in prison until the end of the war.

On April 2, 1865, while President Davis was attending church at St. Paul's Episcopal Church, he received an urgent message from Lee. The Union had broken through, and Richmond should be evacuated. Davis met with his leaders to prepare to abandon the capital. Government documents were piled in the streets and set on fire. Important information and Confederate money were taken to the train station. By 11 P.M., Davis and most of his leaders were headed out of the city on a train.

The city of Richmond, Virginia, burned on April 2, 1865, while soldiers retreated across the James River.

Mobs formed in Richmond, and citizens panicked. People set fire to everything—warehouses, train depots, flour mills, bridges, ships, arsenals, and more—to destroy anything Union soldiers might be able to use. A southwest wind quickly spread the flames until hundreds of buildings were on fire.

Some people fought the fires, and others left the city. The next morning on April 3, 1865, Union soldiers marched into the Capitol and triumphantly raised the American flag over its roof. Then they began helping the citizens of Richmond put out the fires to save the city from total destruction. Elizabeth described the fiery scene:

> *Had it not been for them [the Union], the whole city would have been a map of smouldering ruins. The loss of public and private property was immense. Our beautiful flour mills, the largest in the world and the pride of our city, were destroyed. Square after square of stores, dwelling houses and factories, warehouses, banks, hotels, bridges, all wrapped in fire, filled the sky with clouds of smoke as incense from the land for its deliverance.*

But she also was thrilled that the Confederacy had been defeated. She wrote:

> *What a moment! Avenging wrath appeased in flames! ... Justice, truth, humanity were vindicated [restored]. ...*

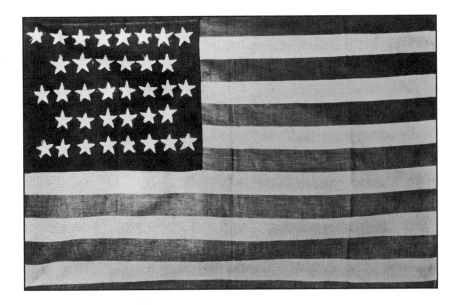

Oh, army of my country, how glorious was your welcome!

The U.S. flag of the Civil War period had 36 stars.

As Richmond burned, Grant remembered the Richmond woman—Elizabeth Van Lew—who had been so valuable to him. She was one of the main reasons there had been a Union victory. He ordered a group of soldiers to go to the Van Lew mansion to protect Elizabeth, her mother, and their home.

When the men arrived, they saw a 25-foot (75-m) American flag hanging in front of her house. However, Elizabeth was not home. She was out on one last spy mission, searching for valuable documents in the ruins of the Confederate War Department building. ℘

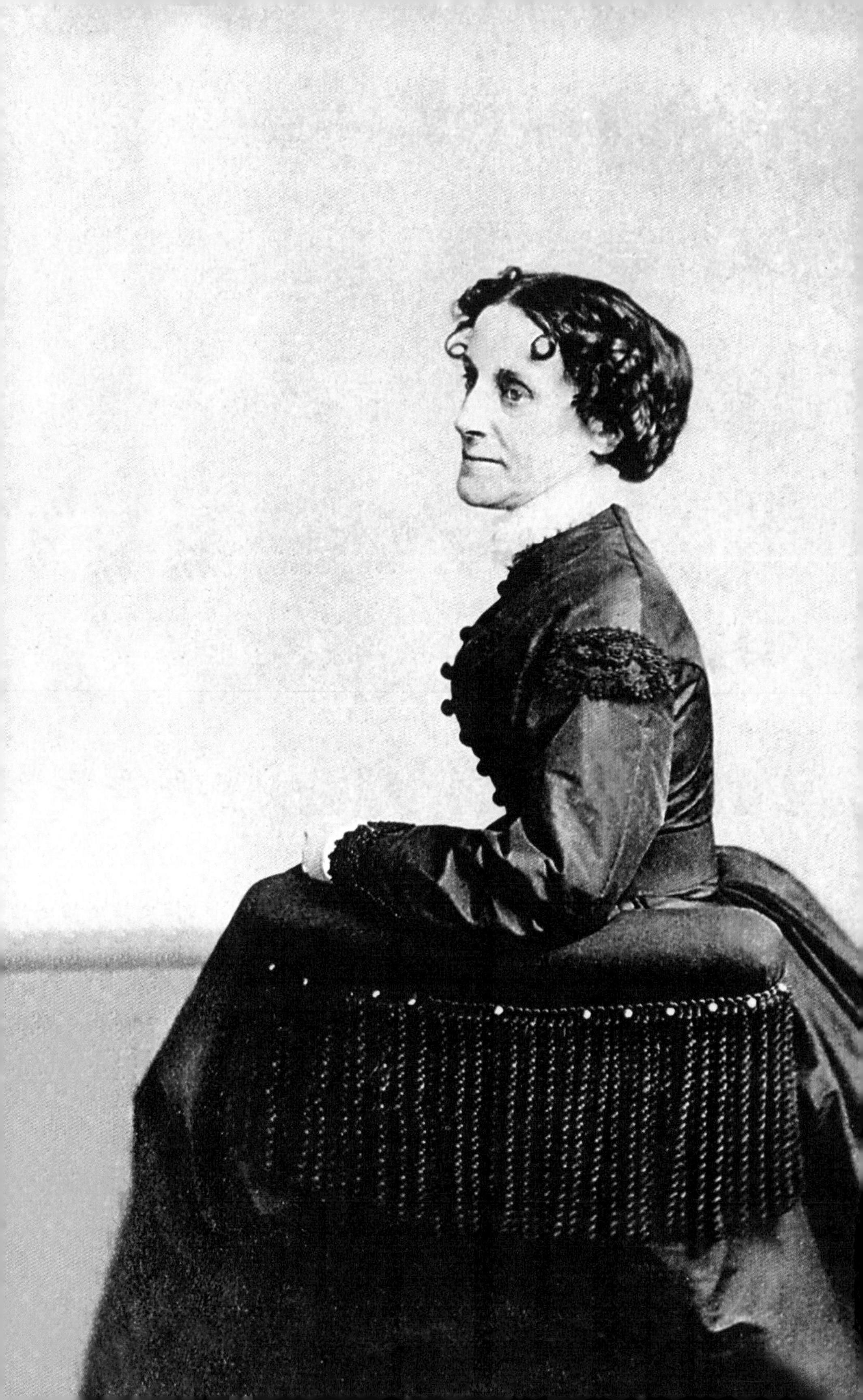

8 SCORNED

Chapter

On April 9, 1865, just a week after Richmond was set on fire, Lee surrendered his Confederate soldiers to Grant. The two generals had agreed to meet in the small village of Appomattox Court House, Virginia, at the home of Wilmer McLean. There they agreed on the terms of a Confederate surrender.

The next day, celebrations broke out in Washington, D.C. Four days later, the American flag was jubilantly raised over Fort Sumter, South Carolina, where the war had begun. That night, however, on April 14, 1865, President Lincoln was assassinated at Ford's Theatre in Washington, D.C.

In May, the remaining Confederate forces surrendered. After four years of fighting, the long war that pitted Americans against Americans—the Civil

War—was finally over.

Elizabeth Van Lew celebrated the victory, and she celebrated what Lincoln and the U.S. Congress had done for slaves. On January 1, 1863, in the midst of the battles, Lincoln had signed the Emancipation Proclamation, freeing all slaves in Confederate states. Two years later, on January 31, 1865, Congress approved the 13th Amendment to the U.S. Constitution, abolishing slavery completely in the entire country.

Elizabeth was happy that slaves were finally free, and she was pleased that the war was over, but she was broke. She had spent a lot of her money on her spy network and for the care of Union prisoners. She had also spent much of her money to purchase slaves, just so she could set them free.

Immediately after the war, Grant approved a payment of $2,000 to the Van Lews to cover their expenses. But that money was soon gone. Elizabeth believed she should receive more for what she had sacrificed for her country.

On April 14, 1865, just five days after the end of the Civil War, John Wilkes Booth shot President Abraham Lincoln. The president was attending a special performance of the comedy, Our American Cousin, at Ford's Theatre in Washington, D.C. At almost the same moment, Lewis Powell attacked William Henry Seward, U.S. secretary of state, slashing his throat twice. However, a surgical collar saved Seward, and he lived another seven years.

Abraham Lincoln and his Emancipation Proclamation

On December 1, 1866, Van Lew asked the U.S. War Department for all papers relating to her intelligence activities during the war. This would be her

Elizabeth Van Lew lived most of her life in Richmond, Virginia.

proof that she had done a great service for the United States and that she should receive some financial reward.

In 1867, intelligence chief Sharpe wrote a long letter to Congress explaining Van Lew's brave and valuable service during the war. He reminded members of Congress of her strong patriotism and encouraged them to approve a payment of $15,000 to the Van Lews.

He wrote to Congress:

> *[F]or a long, long time, she represented*
> *all that was left of the power of the U.S.*
> *government in the city of Richmond.*

Despite high praise from Sharpe, General Grant, and General Butler, Congress approved only $5,000 for Van Lew. Although that was quite a bit of money at that time, it was still not nearly as much as what Sharpe had hoped to give this important Civil War spy.

Elizabeth Van Lew lived in Richmond for almost the rest of her life. But the people of her city never forgot her pro-Union activities, and they never forgave her for turning against her Southern friends. Elizabeth wrote:

> *[I am] held in contempt & scorn by the*
> *narrow minded men and women of my*
> *city for my loyalty. ... Socially living as*
> *utterly alone in the city of my birth, as if*
> *I spoke a different language.*

The more the people of Richmond learned about what Van Lew did during the war, the more they hated and scorned her. ✍

9 HONORED

❧❧❧

The people of Richmond certainly didn't appreciate Elizabeth Van Lew, but one person did—Ulysses S. Grant. In 1869, just two weeks after his inauguration as president of the United States, he appointed 50-year-old Van Lew postmistress of Richmond with a salary of $1,200 a year. She was now in charge of managing the post office. Since the president had appointed her, she had some political power. She would soon discover, however, that the people of Richmond were not happy about her appointment. After all, they considered her a traitor, and many didn't like a woman holding such an important position. They wanted her replaced by a man.

Van Lew ran the Richmond post office very

efficiently for eight years. She improved and modernized it by setting up a delivery system. Instead of coming to the post office to pick up mail, citizens of Richmond now had mail delivered to their houses. They also didn't have to come to the post office to mail a letter. Mailboxes were placed on the main streets so people could mail their letters from several places throughout the city.

Even though Van Lew held a respectable position and improved the postal system, the people of Richmond still did not respect her. When Elizabeth's mother died on September 13, 1875, Elizabeth realized how few friends she had. She wrote to a friend in Boston:

> *I live, and have lived for years, as entirely distinct from the citizens as if I were plague-stricken. ... Rarely, very rarely is our door-bell ever rung by any but a pauper, or those desiring my service. ... September [13], 1875 my mother was taken from me by death. We had not friends enough to be pall-bearers.*

When Grant's second presidential term was almost over in 1877, he recommended that the next U.S. president, Rutherford B. Hayes, re-appoint Van Lew as postmistress of Richmond. But Hayes did not appoint her to the position, and she lost her job in May 1877.

A U.S. postage stamp used in the late 19th century

Van Lew got by on very little money for several years. In 1883, she applied for a job at the U.S. Post Office Department. She was hired as a clerk with a salary of $1,200 a year and moved to Washington, D.C. But four years later, 69-year-old Van Lew was transferred to another department with a salary of only $720 a year. She resigned her position and returned to Richmond.

For the next several years, Van Lew tried to get another job with the U.S. government, but she was unsuccessful. She was disappointed that the government would not help her after all she had done for her country. With no money and no one to help, Van Lew withdrew almost completely from society. When she went out of her house, she was fearful and suspicious of people, which confirmed many people's false belief that she was odd and mentally unstable—"Crazy Bet," as she was called.

*Paul Joseph
Revere (left)
and his brother
Edward Revere*

In desperation, Van Lew turned to the family of Paul Joseph Revere, a Union Army officer she had helped during the war. Revere died in the war in 1863. His brother Edward also served in the war and died in 1862. The Reveres' grandfather was the famous Paul Revere, who rode through Massachusetts warning the colonists that the British were coming during the Revolutionary War. For more than 100 years, the Revere family had been dedicated to their country, and now perhaps they would help Van Lew.

The Reveres appreciated what Van Lew did for their family and their country. John Reynolds, the nephew of Paul Joseph Revere, set up a bank account for Van Lew. Wealthy people from Boston, Massachusetts, deposited money in her account. Most of them were friends or relatives of Union officers Elizabeth had helped at Libby Prison. Reynolds regularly visited Van Lew in Richmond and gave her money from the account, and thus began a lasting friendship.

Now in her 70s, Van Lew had money to live on, but she was also becoming very frail and nervous. When she walked around Richmond, she muttered to herself and acted in strange ways. People called her a witch, young boys made fun of her, and little girls were terrified of her. Parents warned their children that Crazy Bet would get them, if they didn't behave.

The people of Richmond were not kind to Van Lew, and she wanted to move to the North. Her friends and fellow Union supporters had all died or moved away. Her brother John and his family had left Richmond, all except one daughter, Eliza, who stayed to care for her aunt Elizabeth. As much as Van Lew wanted to move,

Elizabeth Van Lew (right) had a meal with her brother, nieces, and nephew in the garden at the Van Lew mansion.

she couldn't sell her Church Hill home. The huge house needed repairs, the gardens were overgrown, and no one was interested in Elizabeth Van Lew's home.

In 1895, John died, and soon after, Elizabeth's sister Anna also died. During the winter of 1899-1900, Elizabeth became ill with dropsy, a sickness that caused her body to fill up with fluids. In May 1900, Eliza also became ill and died unexpectedly. Elizabeth was devastated, and her own health quickly got worse. Now she was completely alone, very sick, and unable to take care of herself. She asked Anna's two daughters to stay with her during her final days, which they agreed to do.

Before she died, she shared with her nieces a secret she had kept for nearly 40 years. Buried in her backyard was her journal, a detailed account of her Union spy activities during the Civil War. Her nieces dug it up and brought it to her. Elizabeth commented with surprise, "Why, there is nearly twice as much more. What has become of it?" No one ever found the rest of her journal.

On September 25, 1900, Elizabeth Van Lew died at the age of 81. She was buried in Shockoe Cemetery in Richmond, near the graves of her mother and father. She left all her property to her niece Annie, her brother John's daughter. She left her journal to John Reynolds, the man who had raised money for her support for almost 20 years.

of all who were of the Brown party. — They thirsted for it; they cried out for it. It was not enough that one old man should die. No plea of feeble intellect, of misguided youth, would be listened to; and when a deputation arrived / waited on to see the Legislature to solicit mercy for the young, one of the raiders, a lady, one of the most highly respectable in the city, implored the members to steel their hearts, to let no appeal, no pity move them! What struck me most painfully in all this was the universal want of humanity towards the raiders. I hold that one spark of the Divine love of Christ in our hearts, gives us a feeling of sympathy with all his creatures, however sunken, however sinning. I never thought John Brown right, but I have always looked upon him as one who suffered so deeply with / from a sense of the wrong of the slave, that his strong

Her grave was unmarked for nearly two years. But Reynolds again started working to help this woman who had helped his family. Soon he arranged for a 2,000-pound (900-kilogram) stone to be

Page two of Elizabeth Van Lew's journal that she buried in her backyard

brought from Boston to Richmond. He designed a bronze plaque for the front of it, which read:

Elizabeth L. Van Lew
1818   1900
She risked everything that is dear to man—friends—fortune—comfort—health—life itself—all for the one absorbing desire of her heart—that slavery might be abolished and the Union preserved. This boulder from the capitol hill in Boston is a tribute from Massachusetts friends

Less than a month after Van Lew died, her mansion was put up for sale at an auction. A civic organization, the Virginia Club, purchased it, but rumors spread that the house was haunted. People reported hearing strange noises and seeing figures appear on the basement wall. Finally, the house was condemned by the city of Richmond and torn down in 1912. Bellevue Elementary School was later built on the site.

How odd that a tribute to a Union spy was placed in a Southern graveyard in Richmond, the capital of the Confederacy.

When Elizabeth Van Lew died, the nation lost someone who cared deeply about uniting her country and believed that all people who lived there should be free. Van Lew once wrote on a small scrap of paper:

For my loyalty to my country I have two beautiful names—here I am called "Traitor," farther north a "Spy"—instead of the honored name of Faithful.

To Elizabeth Van Lew, she was neither a traitor nor a spy—she was a woman who wanted to be remembered as faithful and loyal to her country, the United States of America. ❧

Headstone for the grave of Elizabeth Van Lew in Shockoe Cemetery, Richmond, Virginia

VAN LEW'S LIFE

1830s

Attends private
school in
Philadelphia,
Pennsylvania

1818

Born in
Richmond,
Virginia,
October 15

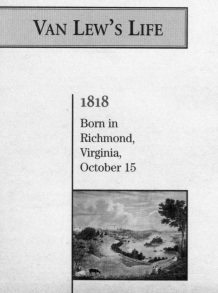

1843

Father John Van
Lew dies

1815

1840

1840

Auguste Rodin,
famous sculptor
of *The Thinker*,
is born

1827

Modern-day
matches are
invented by coat-
ing the end of a
wooden stick
with phosphorus

WORLD EVENTS

1851

Abolitionist
Fredrika Bremer
visits the Van Lews

1860

Supports Abraham
Lincoln for
president of the
United States

1861

Supports the Union
while living in a
Confederate State
during the Civil War

1855

1852

Postage stamps
are widely used

1860

Austrian composer
Gustav Mahler is
born in Kalischt
(now in Austria)

VAN LEW'S LIFE

1862

Begins work
in prisons

1863

Becomes an agent
for the govern-
ment of the
United States

1864

Plans recovery of
Ulric Dahlgren's
body from
Richmond grave-
yard; prepares for
Libby Prison escape

1862

West Virginia
is created

1863

Thomas Nast
draws the modern
Santa Claus for
Harper's Weekly

WORLD EVENTS

1865

Watches Richmond,
Virginia, burn as
Conferate soldiers
leave the city

1866

Asks the U.S. War
Department for
papers relating to
her spy activities

1865

1865

Lewis Carroll writes
*Alice's Adventures in
Wonderland*

VAN LEW'S LIFE

1867
U.S. Congress approves $5,000 to be given to Van Lew

1869
Appointed postmistress of Richmond by President Grant

1875
Mother Eliza Baker Van Lew dies

1870

1869
The periodic table of elements is invented by Dimitri Mendeleyev

1873
Typewriters get the QWERTY keyboard

1876
Alexander Graham Bell uses the first telephone to speak to his assistant, Thomas Watson

WORLD EVENTS

1883

Works as clerk for the U.S. Post Office Department in Washington, D.C.

1900

Dies in Richmond, Virginia, September 25

1900

1886

Grover Cleveland dedicates the Statue of Liberty in New York, a gift from the people of France

1883

The first skyscraper, 10 stories, is built in Chicago

DATE OF BIRTH: October 15, 1818

BIRTHPLACE: Richmond, Virginia

FATHER: John Van Lew (1790–1843)

MOTHER: Eliza Louise Baker Van
Lew (1798–1875)

SIBLINGS: Anna Van Lew Klapp
(dates unknown)
John Van Lew (?–1895)

EDUCATION: Private school in
Philadelphia, Pennsylvania

DATE OF DEATH: September 25, 1900

PLACE OF BURIAL: Shockoe Cemetery,
Richmond, Virginia

Additional Resources

IN THE LIBRARY

Caravantes, Peggy. *Petticoat Spies: Six Women Spies of the Civil War.* Greensboro, N.C.: Morgan Reynolds Publishing, 2002.

Lyons, Mary E., and Muriel Branch. *Dear Ellen Bee: A Civil War Scrapbook of Two Union Spies.* New York: Atheneum Books for Young Readers, 2000.

Raatma, Lucia. *Great Women of the Civil War.* Minneapolis: Compass Point Books, 2005.

Zeinert, Karen. *Elizabeth Van Lew: Southern Belle, Union Spy.* Minneapolis: Dillon Press, 1995.

LOOK FOR MORE SIGNATURE LIVES
BOOKS ABOUT THIS ERA:

Jefferson Davis: *President of the Confederate States of America*

Frederick Douglass: *Slave, Writer, Abolitionist*

William Lloyd Garrison: *Abolitionist and Journalist*

Ulysses S. Grant: *Union General and U.S. President*

Thomas "Stonewall" Jackson: *Confederate General*

Robert E. Lee: *Confederate Commander*

Abraham Lincoln: *Great American President*

Harriet Beecher Stowe: *Author and Advocate*

ON THE WEB

For more information on *Elizabeth Van Lew*, use FactHound to track down Web sites related to this book.

1. Go to *www.facthound.com*
2. Type in a search word related to this book or this book ID: 0756509858
3. Click on the *Fetch It* button.

FactHound will find the best
Web sites for you.

HISTORIC SITES

Virginia Historical Society
428 North Blvd.
Richmond, VA 23220
804/358-4901
To view an album kept by Van Lew containing correspondence and documents about her life

The Museum of the Confederacy
1201 E. Clay St.
Richmond, VA 23219
804/649-1861
To tour the Confederate White House

abolitionist
a person who worked to get rid of slavery

bribe
money or gift given to someone to influence the
person's judgment or decision

burlap
a coarse fabric used for bagging or wrapping
heavy items

cipher
a code that uses letters or symbols to represent
letters of the alphabet

Confederate
a person who supported the cause of the
Confederate States of America

eccentric
different than what is accepted as normal; odd
or peculiar

photographic
capable of retaining information as accurate and
detailed as a photograph

rebel
Confederate Army soldier during the Civil War

undercover
done in secret, especially in spying activities

underground
concealed and done in secret

Union
the Northern states that fought against the
Southern states in the Civil War

Yankee
Union Army soldier during the Civil War

Source Notes

Chapter 3

Page 29, line 15: Elizabeth R. Varon. *Southern Lady, Yankee Spy: The True Story of Elizabeth Van Lew, A Union Agent in the Heart of the Confederacy.* New York: Oxford University Press, 2003, p. 23.

Page 31, line 25: David D. Ryan, ed. *A Yankee Spy in Richmond: The Civil War Diary of "Crazy Bet" Van Lew.* Mechanicsburg, Penn.: Stackpole Books, 1996, pp. 28-29.

Chapter 4

Page 35, line 10: Ibid., pp. 32-33.

Page 36, line 17: Ibid., p. 32.

Page 36, line 19: Ibid., p. 32.

Page 40, line 11: Ibid., p. 43.

Page 40, line 20: Ibid., p. 44.

Page 42, line 24: *Southern Lady, Yankee Spy: The True Story of Elizabeth Van Lew, A Union Agent in the Heart of the Confederacy*, p. 56.

Page 44, line 8: Colonel George H. Sharpe's Recommendation, January, 1867, from the Van Lew Papers

Page 47, line 12: *Southern Lady, Yankee Spy: The True Story of Elizabeth Van Lew, A Union Agent in the Heart of the Confederacy*, pp. 59-60.

Page 48, line 10: Ibid., p. 60.

Chapter 5

Page 54, line 21: Ibid., p. 90.

Chapter 6

Page 62, line 19: *A Yankee Spy in Richmond: The Civil War Diary of "Crazy Bet" Van Lew.* pp. 59-60.

Page 63, line 9: Ibid., p. 59.

Page 64, line 18: *Southern Lady, Yankee Spy: The True Story of Elizabeth Van Lew, A Union Agent in the Heart of the Confederacy*, p. 133.

Page 66, line 1: *A Yankee Spy in Richmond: The Civil War Diary of "Crazy Bet" Van Lew.* p. 56.

Page 69, line 11: Ibid., p. 72.

Chapter 7

Page 71, line 2: Ibid., p. 25.

Page 71, line 7: Ibid., p. 97.

Page 72, line 6: Ibid., p. 54.

Page 73, line 6: Ibid., pp. 94-95.

Page 75, line 5: *Southern Lady, Yankee Spy: The True Story of Elizabeth Van Lew, A Union Agent in the Heart of the Confederacy*, p. 133.

Page 76, line 10: *A Yankee Spy in Richmond: The Civil War Diary of "Crazy Bet" Van Lew*. p. 108.

Page 78, line 14: *Southern Lady, Yankee Spy: The True Story of Elizabeth Van Lew, A Union Agent in the Heart of the Confederacy*, p. 194.

Page 78, line 27: Ibid., p. 191.

Chapter 8

Page 85, line 2: *A Yankee Spy in Richmond: The Civil War Diary of "Crazy Bet" Van Lew*. pp. 115-116.

Page 85, line 16: Ibid., p. 129.

Chapter 9

Page 88, line 15: Ibid., p. 20.

Page 92, line 19: *Southern Lady, Yankee Spy: The True Story of Elizabeth Van Lew, A Union Agent in the Heart of the Confederacy*, p. 251.

Page 94, line 26: *Civil War Richmond.*
www.mdgorman.com/Other%20Sites/Miss%20Van%20Lew.htm, 2004.

Burns, Ken. "The Civil War." *PBS.org.* www.pbs.org/civilwar.

Clasen, Nancy Jean. *Elizabeth Louise Van Lew, Civil War Unionist and Abolitionist: Leader of the Richmond Union Underground* [doctoral thesis]. Mankato, Minn., 1978.

"Elizabeth Van Lew." *Home of the American Civil War.* www.civilwarhome.com/vanlewbio.htm.

Nolan, Jeannette Covert. *Yankee Spy: Elizabeth Van Lew.* New York: J. Messner, 1970.

"Richmond." *National Park Service.* www.nps.gov/rich.

Ryan, David D., ed. *A Yankee Spy in Richmond: The Civil War Diary of "Crazy Bet" Van Lew.* Mechanicsburg, Penn.: Stackpole Books, 1996.

Varon, Elizabeth R. *Southern Lady, Yankee Spy: The True Story of Elizabeth Van Lew, A Union Agent in the Heart of the Confederacy.* New York: Oxford University Press, 2003.

Heidi Schoof was an elementary school teacher before pursuing her dream of writing and editing books for children. She loves to read books for all ages and especially enjoys researching historical subjects through old photos. Heidi lives with her husband and six active children in New Ulm, Minnesota.

Image Credits